STATE PROFILES
ALABAMA

BY PATRICK PERISH

BELLWETHER MEDIA • MINNEAPOLIS, MN

Blastoff! Discovery launches a new mission: reading to learn. Filled with facts and features, each book offers you an exciting new world to explore!

BLASTOFF! UNIVERSE

BLASTOFF! Beginners — GRADE K

BLASTOFF! READERS — GRADES 1-3

BLASTOFF! DISCOVERY — GRADE 4

This edition first published in 2022 by Bellwether Media, Inc.

No part of this publication may be reproduced in whole or in part without written permission of the publisher.
For information regarding permission, write to Bellwether Media, Inc., Attention: Permissions Department,
6012 Blue Circle Drive, Minnetonka, MN 55343.

Library of Congress Cataloging-in-Publication Data

Names: Perish, Patrick, author.
Title: Alabama / by Patrick Perish.
Description: Minneapolis, MN : Bellwether Media, Inc., 2022. | Series: Blastoff! Discovery: State profiles | Includes bibliographical references and index. | Audience: Ages 7-13 | Audience: Grades 4-6 | Summary: "Engaging images accompany information about Alabama. The combination of high-interest subject matter and narrative text is intended for students in grades 3 through 8"– Provided by publisher.
Identifiers: LCCN 2021019683 (print) | LCCN 2021019684 (ebook) | ISBN 9781644873724 (library binding) | ISBN 9781648341496 (ebook)
Subjects: LCSH: Alabama–Juvenile literature.
Classification: LCC F326.3 .P47 2022 (print) | LCC F326.3 (ebook) | DDC 976.1–dc23
LC record available at https://lccn.loc.gov/2021019683
LC ebook record available at https://lccn.loc.gov/2021019684

Editor: Colleen Sexton   Designer: Brittany McIntosh

Printed in the United States of America, North Mankato, MN.

TABLE OF CONTENTS

In the morning light, a boat motor roars to life. A family is taking a fishing trip. Their guide steers the boat onto the dark waters of Mobile Bay. The family readies their rods and waits for fish. They watch long-legged shorebirds hunt for crabs and shrimp in the shallows. Suddenly, a line pulls tight. A bite!

IT'S A JUBILEE!

Sometimes huge numbers of fish and shellfish swarm the shores of Mobile Bay. Locals call these events jubilees. The plentiful seafood is a cause for feasting and celebration.

CATHEDRAL CAVERNS STATE PARK

CHEAHA MOUNTAIN

CIVIL RIGHTS MEMORIAL CENTER

U.S. SPACE & ROCKET CENTER

After landing several fish, the boat heads for shore. The bay is bustling. Boats zigzag across the open water. The inviting smell of grilled meals drifts through the air. On a far-off beach, workers raise colorful tents as crowds gather for a festival. Welcome to Alabama!

Alabama is in the southeastern United States. This long, narrow state covers 52,420 square miles (135,767 square kilometers). Mississippi is Alabama's western neighbor. Tennessee lies to the north. Georgia borders Alabama to the east. Florida lies to the south. Alabama's southwestern corner reaches the **Gulf** of Mexico. Mobile Bay cuts into this 53-mile (85-kilometer) shoreline. Many islands in the Gulf also belong to Alabama.

Montgomery is the capital of Alabama. It sits on the Alabama River near the center of the state. To the north is Birmingham, Alabama's largest city. Other important cities include Huntsville and Mobile.

MISSISSIPPI

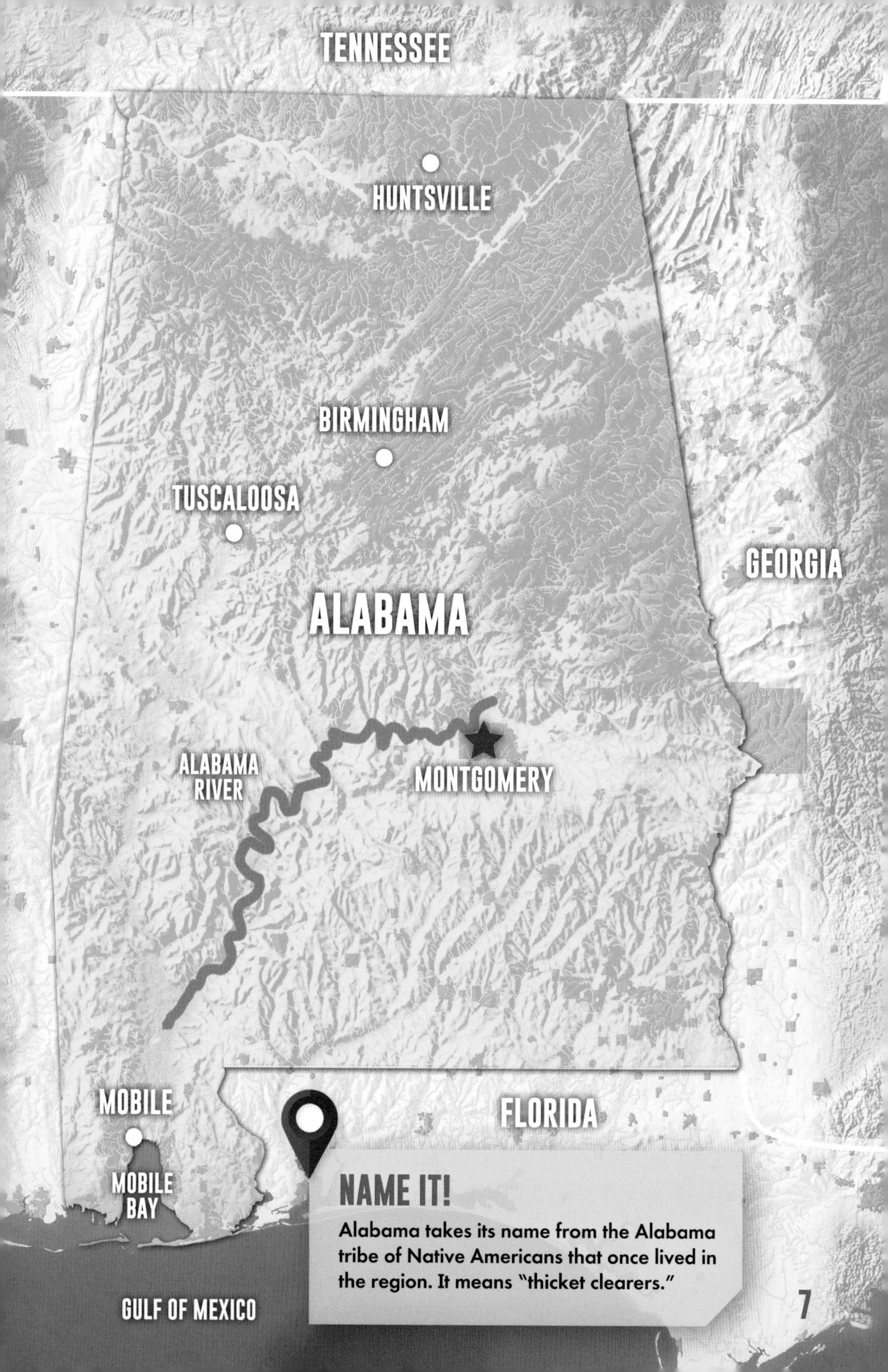

TENNESSEE

HUNTSVILLE

BIRMINGHAM

TUSCALOOSA

GEORGIA

ALABAMA

ALABAMA
RIVER

MONTGOMERY

MOBILE

FLORIDA

MOBILE
BAY

NAME IT!

Alabama takes its name from the Alabama tribe of Native Americans that once lived in the region. It means "thicket clearers."

GULF OF MEXICO

RUSSELL CAVE

RUSSELL CAVE

Early peoples took shelter in Russell Cave in northeastern Alabama. They left behind tools and weapons that provide a glimpse into life thousands of years ago.

People have lived in Alabama for about 12,000 years. Many Native American tribes formed. They included the Chickasaw, Creek, Choctaw, and Cherokee. After Europeans arrived in the 1500s, the French, British, and Spanish struggled to control the area. The French established the first permanent European **settlement** near the Mobile River in 1702. All of Alabama was under U.S. control by 1813. In 1819, it became the 22nd state.

In the 1830s, the U.S. government forced out Native Americans. White settlers came, many bringing **enslaved** Africans to work their large farms. Alabama fought for the **Confederacy** during the **Civil War** from 1861 to 1865.

NATIVE PEOPLES OF ALABAMA

CREEK PEOPLE

- Original lands in Alabama and Georgia
- About 2,300 Poarch Creek Indians in Alabama today
- Also called Muskogee

CHOCTAW PEOPLE

- Original lands in Mississippi and western Alabama
- About 3,600 members of the MOWA band of Choctaw in Alabama today

CHICKASAW PEOPLE

- Original lands in northern Mississippi, southwestern Tennessee, and northwestern Alabama
- Relocated to Oklahoma in the 1800s, where they live today

CHEROKEE PEOPLE

- Original lands in Georgia, South Carolina, North Carolina, and Tennessee, but they were moved to Alabama in the 1700s
- Relocated in the 1800s
- Many live in Oklahoma and North Carolina today

Alabama's landscape is varied and beautiful. The Appalachian Mountains dip into northern Alabama. Quick-flowing streams wind through these tree-covered peaks. Southern Alabama is part of the Coastal Plain region. Rich soil covers the flat landscape. This region contains the **Black Belt**. Crops thrive in this strip of rolling farmland. Swamps, **bayous**, and sandy beaches line Alabama's coast.

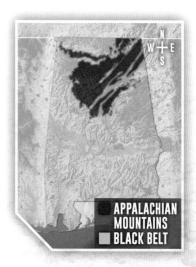

APPALACHIAN MOUNTAINS
BLACK BELT

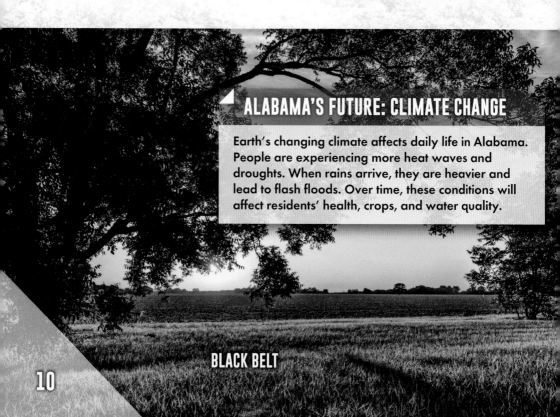

ALABAMA'S FUTURE: CLIMATE CHANGE

Earth's changing climate affects daily life in Alabama. People are experiencing more heat waves and droughts. When rains arrive, they are heavier and lead to flash floods. Over time, these conditions will affect residents' health, crops, and water quality.

BLACK BELT

APPALACHIAN
MOUNTAINS

SPRING
HIGH: 74°F (23°C)
LOW: 54°F (12°C)

SUMMER
HIGH: 90°F (32°C)
LOW: 71°F (22°C)

FALL
HIGH: 76°F (24°C)
LOW: 56°F (13°C)

WINTER
HIGH: 57°F (14°C)
LOW: 39°F (4°C)

°F = degrees Fahrenheit
°C = degrees Celsius

Alabama has a warm, **humid** climate. Winters are mild.
Long summers make for long growing seasons. **Hurricanes**
sometimes batter the coast. They can bring heavy rains
inland, causing floods. Northern Alabama often experiences
severe storms and even tornadoes.

COPPERHEAD SNAKE

BLACK BEAR

AMERICAN ALLIGATOR

BULL SHARK

Alabama has some of the greatest **biodiversity** in the country. In Appalachian forests, northern flickers, also called yellowhammers, fly from tree to tree. Mountain streams are home to colorful darters and native mussels. Copperhead snakes wait between rocks for mice and lizards. In Dismals Canyon, thousands of glowworms light up the night.

Pine forests are home to black bears and insect-eating pitcher plants. Wading egrets hunt for fish and frogs in swamps while turtles and alligators bask nearby. Manatees and bull sharks swim near the coast. Blind, colorless fish and crayfish live in Alabama's caves.

NORTHERN FLICKER

Alabama has the third-most endangered species in the country. Many are water creatures. Water runoff leaves harmful waste in rivers and lakes. Some Alabamians are working to protect these habitats. Even so, many species are at risk of disappearing.

ALABAMA RED-BELLIED TURTLE

Life Span: about 50 years
Status: endangered

Alabama red-bellied turtle range =

LEAST CONCERN	NEAR THREATENED	VULNERABLE	ENDANGERED	CRITICALLY ENDANGERED	EXTINCT IN THE WILD	EXTINCT

Alabama has a population of about 5 million people. Around 6 of every 10 Alabamians live in **urban** areas. The largest are the cities of Birmingham, Huntsville, and Montgomery and their **suburbs**.

BIRMINGHAM

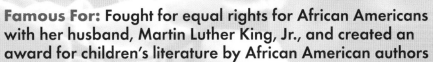

FAMOUS ALABAMIAN

Name: Coretta Scott King
Born: April 27, 1927
Died: January 30, 2006
Hometown: Marion, Alabama
Famous For: Fought for equal rights for African Americans with her husband, Martin Luther King, Jr., and created an award for children's literature by African American authors

Alabama's early settlers were English, Irish, and German. Today, Alabamians come from many different backgrounds. Most Alabamians have European **ancestors**. About one in four Alabamians are Black or African American. Smaller numbers are Hispanic and Asian. Native

Americans include the Poarch Creek Indians and the MOWA Band of Choctaw in southern Alabama. **Immigrants** make up a growing portion of Alabama's population. Many newcomers came from Mexico, Guatemala, India, and Korea.

ROSA PARKS MONUMENT

Montgomery was founded in 1819 near the Alabama River. It became the state capital in 1846 and served as the first capital of the Confederate States in 1861. In the 1950s and 60s, Montgomery became the heart of the **civil rights movement**.

A BUS BOYCOTT

In 1955, Rosa Parks was arrested in Montgomery. She refused to give up her bus seat to a white man. African Americans protested and refused to ride city buses. Their actions ended segregation on city buses.

Today, Montgomery is the state's second-largest city. Maxwell Air Force Base is its largest employer. Montgomery is a **cultural** center. The Alabama Shakespeare Festival draws crowds every year. Visitors to the W.A. Gayle Planetarium explore outer space. The National Memorial for Peace and Justice highlights the history of Black people from slavery to **segregation** to present day.

NATIONAL MEMORIAL
FOR PEACE AND JUSTICE

COTTON FIELD

Alabama's **natural resources** shaped the state's early industries. Iron ore and coal mining led to a strong steel industry. Forests provided timber for paper products. Rich soil supported farming. Cotton was the chief crop for decades. Then in 1915, insects called boll weevils destroyed the cotton fields. George Washington Carver and other scientists helped farmers grow new crops such as peanuts and soybeans.

WHAT A PEST!

A statue honoring the boll weevil stands in the city of Enterprise, Alabama. It is a reminder of how farmers and scientists turned a disaster into an opportunity.

Today, cotton is a leading farm product again, along with poultry and peanuts. Factory workers make cars, airplane parts, and chemicals. Huntsville is an important center for technology research. Most Alabamians have **service jobs**. Many work in stores, hospitals, and banks.

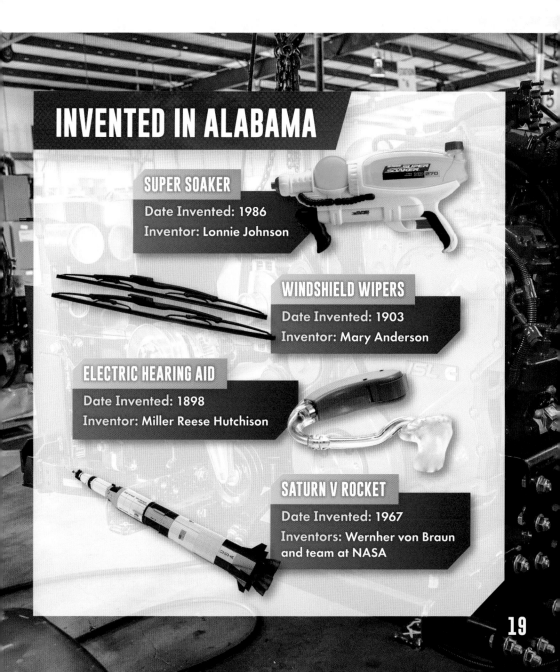

INVENTED IN ALABAMA

SUPER SOAKER
Date Invented: 1986
Inventor: Lonnie Johnson

WINDSHIELD WIPERS
Date Invented: 1903
Inventor: Mary Anderson

ELECTRIC HEARING AID
Date Invented: 1898
Inventor: Miller Reese Hutchison

SATURN V ROCKET
Date Invented: 1967
Inventors: Wernher von Braun and team at NASA

SHRIMP AND GRITS

Alabama's favorite dishes have deep roots. Corn introduced by Native Americans features in grits and cornbread. European settlers brought pork. Barbecue became a popular way to prepare this meat. Alabamians serve smoked pork on a bun topped with coleslaw or pickles.

SMOKED PORK SANDWICH

Cooks near the coast serve up gumbo, shrimp and grits, and other seafood dishes. Fried green tomatoes and fried okra are common side dishes. Enslaved Africans introduced okra along with peanuts and black-eyed peas. Sweet treats include banana pudding and chocolate marshmallow cookies called MoonPies. The Lane cake is the official dessert of Alabama. It features layers of coconut, pecans, and raisins.

MOONPIE OVER MOBILE

Mobile counts down to the New Year by dropping an electric MoonPie. A fresh-baked version is also cut up and served to the crowd. It is the world's largest MoonPie!

FRIED GREEN TOMATOES

4-6 SERVINGS

Have an adult help you make this popular side dish!

INGREDIENTS

4 to 6 green tomatoes
salt and pepper
cornmeal
bacon grease or vegetable oil

DIRECTIONS

1. Slice the tomatoes into 1/4- to 1/2-inch (1/2- to 1-centimeter) slices.

2. Sprinkle with salt and pepper.

3. Dip in cornmeal and fry in hot grease or oil for about 3 minutes or until golden on the bottom.

4. Gently turn and fry the other side.

TALLADEGA SUPERSPEEDWAY

Alabama is home to two legendary college football teams. The Auburn Tigers and the University of Alabama Crimson Tide compete every year in the Iron Bowl. Fans of stock car racing head to the Talladega Superspeedway. It is the longest NASCAR track.

GONE FISHING

Mobile Bay's Deep Sea Fish Rodeo is held every July. It is the country's oldest saltwater fishing competition!

Hunting and fishing have a long history in Alabama. Deer and turkeys are popular game animals. Residents enjoy hiking and kayaking in the state's parks. Alabama's many caves are great for exploring. The state also offers a lively arts scene. Theater productions and folk art festivals draw many visitors. Concerts showcase everything from country rock to the blues.

CAVE EXPLORING

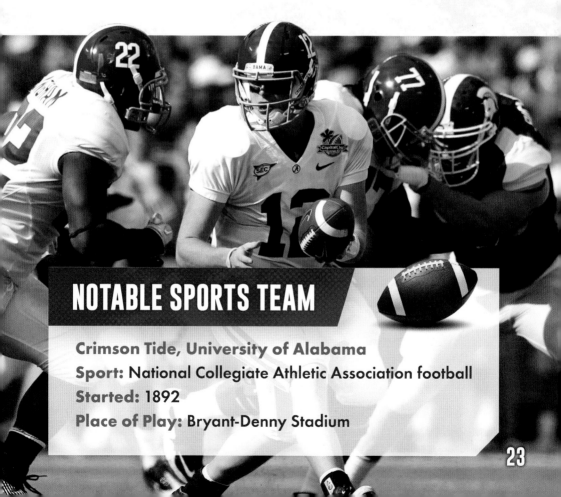

NOTABLE SPORTS TEAM

Crimson Tide, University of Alabama
Sport: National Collegiate Athletic Association football
Started: 1892
Place of Play: Bryant-Denny Stadium

Alabama's festivals celebrate the state's rich culture. The Moundville Native American Festival in October features the arts, crafts, and **traditions** of southeastern tribes. Skilled musicians also gather in October to compete at the Tennessee Valley Old Time Fiddlers Convention. It honors Alabama's musical roots.

Food festivals bring people together. Thousands flock to Gulf Shores in October for its Shrimp Festival. Dothan hosts the National Peanut Festival each November. It features a carnival, live music, and a lot of peanuts. Mobile is home to America's oldest Mardi Gras celebration. People line the streets to watch colorful floats on parade. There is plenty to celebrate in Alabama!

SHRIMP FESTIVAL
GULF SHORES

MARDI GRAS
MOBILE

1120
Early peoples begin building Moundville, a large prehistoric city located in what is now western Alabama

1702
French settlers build Fort Louis on the Mobile River, the first capital of French Louisiana

1813
The United States takes southern Alabama from Spain

1540
Explorer Hernando de Soto reaches Alabama

1783
The Revolutionary War ends, and British-controlled northern Alabama becomes part of the United States

1955

The Montgomery bus boycott helps end segregated transportation

1819

Alabama becomes the 22nd state

2010

The Deepwater Horizon oil spill harms wildlife off of Alabama's Gulf coast

1865

The North defeats the South in the Civil War, leading Alabama to officially rejoin the Union in 1868

1969

A rocket designed in Huntsville carries humans to the moon for the first time

Nicknames: The Yellowhammer State, The Heart of Dixie, The Cotton State

Motto: *Audemus jura nostra defendere* (We Dare Defend Our Rights)

Date of Statehood: December 14, 1819 (the 22nd state)

Capital City: Montgomery ★

Other Major Cities: Birmingham, Huntsville, Mobile, Tuscaloosa

Area: 52,420 square miles (135,767 square kilometers); Alabama is the 30th largest state.

Population

5,024,279 (2020)

STATE FLAG

Adopted in 1895, Alabama's flag has a white background. It features a red X called the Cross of St. Andrew. The flag resembles Confederate flags flown during the Civil War.

INDUSTRY

Main Exports

chemicals

minerals

cars and
car parts

paper
products

MANUFACTURING
10%

FARMING AND
NATURAL
RESOURCES
2%

JOBS

GOVERNMENT
15%

SERVICES
73%

Natural Resources
timber, limestone, marble,
iron ore, coal, natural gas, oil

GOVERNMENT

Federal Government

7 REPRESENTATIVES | **2** SENATORS

9 ELECTORAL VOTES

USA

AL

State Government

105 REPRESENTATIVES | **35** SENATORS

STATE SYMBOLS

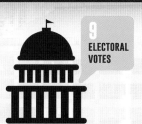

STATE BIRD
YELLOWHAMMER

STATE ANIMAL
BLACK BEAR

STATE FLOWER
CAMELLIA

STATE TREE
SOUTHERN LONGLEAF PINE

ancestors—relatives who lived long ago

bayous—slow-moving streams of water in marshy areas

biodiversity—the variety of life found in a certain place

Black Belt—a strip of rich farmland in Alabama and Mississippi known for growing cotton

civil rights movement—efforts by African Americans to gain equal rights under the law in the 1950s and 1960s

Civil War—a war between the Northern (Union) and Southern (Confederate) states that lasted from 1861 to 1865

Confederacy—the group of Southern states that formed a new country in the early 1860s; the Confederacy fought against the Northern states during the Civil War.

cultural—relating to the beliefs, arts, and ways of life in a place or society

enslaved—to be considered property and forced to work for no pay

gulf—part of an ocean or sea that extends into land

humid—having a lot of moisture in the air

hurricanes—storms formed in the tropics that have violent winds and often have rain and lightning

immigrants—people who move to a new country

natural resources—materials in the earth that are taken out and used to make products or fuel

segregation—the act of separating people based on their race

service jobs—jobs that perform tasks for people or businesses

settlement—a place where newly arrived people live

suburbs—towns and communities just outside of a large city

traditions—customs, ideas, or beliefs handed down from one generation to the next

urban—related to cities and city life

AT THE LIBRARY

Hamilton, John. *Alabama: The Yellowhammer State.* Minneapolis, Minn.: Abdo and Daughters, 2017.

Kittinger, Jo S. *Alabama.* New York, N.Y.: Children's Press, 2018.

Otfinoski, Steven. *The Selma Marches for Civil Rights: We Shall Overcome.* North Mankato, Minn.: Capstone Press, 2019.

ON THE WEB

FACTSURFER

Factsurfer.com gives you a safe, fun way to find more information.

1. Go to www.factsurfer.com.

2. Enter "Alabama" into the search box and click 🔍.

3. Select your book cover to see a list of related content.

INDEX